T0157771

Road
to
Domination

Dion Allen

iUniverse, Inc.
Bloomington

Road to Domination

iUniverse books may be ordered through booksellers or by contacting:

iUniverse
1663 Liberty Drive
Bloomington, IN 47403
www.iuniverse.com
1-800-Authors (1-800-288-4677)

ISBN: 978-1-4502-8691-6 (sc)
ISBN: 978-1-4502-8692-3 (ebk)

Printed in the United States of America

iUniverse rev. date: 1/13/2011

CHAPTER 1

WHY DO THEY DOMINATE?

BY: DION ALLEN

Have you ever wondered why some races seem to excel in life more so than others in the United States? Furthermore, certain races seem to dominate globally more so than other races. Is it because certain races are genetically superior like the Nazis thought? Or is it that certain races are chosen by God to be superior. I do not think that either of these theories are true however there are certain characteristics that have remained with certain races throughout history that have greatly affected their success and domination in the world. This is not a book on superiority. When you read it, keep in mind that it is full of generalizations about each race. It is not meant to infer that any race is superior to another.

If anything it can be used as a self help book. The principles expressed in this book can be utilized by any race or culture in order to improve their position socially and financially in life. This book is broken down into

3 parts. I have developed a theory that focuses on ten characteristics of each race

Parts of the book

1. All of the characteristics are listed and described. There are ten distinct characteristics that are essential for the domination of any race.
2. Each race is analyzed based on each of the ten characteristics.
3. Finally the races are scored on a scale from 1 to 100 and it is then explained why one race tends to dominate more so than others.

The characteristics are:

1. Knowledge of global and local environment
2. Knowledge of science, astronomy and mathematics
3. Organization
4. Aggression
5. Willingness to inflict cruelty
6. Knowledge of religion
7. Natural Physical Ability
8. Knowledge of racial history and culture
9. Racial Unity
10. Business skills

Domination Chart

	European	African	Hispanic	Jewish	Middle-Eastern	Asian	Native American
Knowledge of global and local environment	10	8	6	10	10	10	5
Knowledge of science, astronomy and mathematics	10	8	6	10	10	10	5
Organization	10	7	6	9	6	9	7
Aggression	10	8	7	6	10	9	7
Willingness to inflict cruelty	9	7	7	8	10	9	7
Knowledge of religion	9	7	6	10	10	6	5
Natural Physical Ability	8	10	7	7	6	6	7
Knowledge of history and culture	9	6	8	10	10	8	8
Racial Unity	9	4	10	10	10	8	10
Business skills	10	8	8	10	10	10	8
Total	**94**	**73**	**71**	**90**	**92**	**85**	**69**

Chapter 2

Knowledge of global and local environment

The first characteristic is knowledge of environment. What does this mean? In order to become dominant in the world you must know different characteristics of the Earth. Less than 600 years ago many people thought the Earth was flat. Christopher Columbus proved this theory wrong in 1492. This was a crucial point in history. It is this type of awareness and curiosity of our local and global environment that is crucial in the domination of the world.

CHAPTER 3

KNOWLEDGE OF SCIENCE, ASTRONOMY AND MATHEMATICS

Once a race has an understanding of their environment they can now focus on developing it with the use of science and mathematics. By properly using the sciences, structures such as bridges, houses and businesses may be built. The use of science can also be used to create weapons for protection of the race and for domination of other races.

CHAPTER 4

ORGANIZATION AND STRUCTURE

Now that a race has an understanding of their environment and the science that govern their environment, they can now focus on organizing their civilization. i.e. writing laws, setting up schools, etc..

CHAPTER 5

AGGRESSION

Although aggression might not be the most attractive characteristic it is one of the most essential. Once a society has been established, a certain level of aggression must exist in order to enforce the rules and laws. In addition aggression must exist in order to go to faraway lands and influence others to abide by their rules and their way of thinking.

CHAPTER 6

WILLINGNESS TO INFLICT CRUELTY

Although all races have the ability to inflict violence and cruelty all races are not willing use it. It is inevitable that somewhere along the line resistance will develop. In order to dominate a race has to be willing to inflict cruelty to their own race and other races that are in the way of their domination.

Chapter 7

Knowledge of religion

Whether you agree with a religion or not it is very important that you are knowledgeable of religion. Religion dominates the world. Did you know that most of the wars in the world in some way have a religious basis? Just as important as science and mathematics are, religion is just as important.

CHAPTER 8

NATURAL PHYSICAL ABILITY

Although there are exceptions, there is no doubt that certain races are naturally physically bigger and stronger. Certain races tend to excel more in sports and entertainment such as singing and dancing than others.

CHAPTER 9

KNOWLEDGE OF HISTORY AND CULTURE

Someone once said that you must know where you have been in order to know where you are going. That statement could not be more true. This book will reflect that the races that have a stronger culture belief and knowledge of their ancestors tend to excel in the world. Not only must you know your races history, you must know the history of the world.

CHAPTER 10

RACIAL UNITY

Without racial unity a race cannot survive. While all races have experienced violence within, the races that tend to thrive are the ones that have unity.

CHAPTER 11

BUSINESS SKILLS

Finally, a race must know how to make money. Nothing moves on this planet without money behind it. Certain races seem to have a knack to make money while others are either unable or disinterested in it.

CHAPTER 12

THE AFRICAN

KNOWLEDGE OF ENVIRONMENT

Africa is where the world began. It is often called the mother land. Although African societies were the first societies on Earth, they existed with little or no knowledge of the rest of the world. They were never known to be explorers or sailors abroad. Africans have now migrated around the world however the disinterest in the environment remains.

KNOWLEDGE OF SCIENCE

African's have always excelled in the areas of science, mathematics and astronomy. The Egyptians were some of the greatest thinkers, scientist and engineers in history. This is expressed by architecture such as the pyramids. Even modern day scientist cannot understand how such complicated structures could have been built in that time period.

Organization and Structure

While Africans have excelled in knowledge, they have for centuries displayed an inability to organize. Despite the great intelligence that exists in the African community, there has always existed an inability to maintain organization and structure. This characteristic is even displayed today by the high rate of black on black crime in the United States.

Throughout the continent of Africa there has always been turmoil and instability of governments. The same inability has transcended into African descendents around the world. For example, the African American family unit is in turmoil. The structure that exists in other races family unit does not exist within the African American family unit.

AGGRESSION

African's have been known throughout history as natural warriors. Dating as far back as the Egyptians and the Zulus in Africa, African's have proven to have been some of the greatest natural warriors ever. The inner strength that is present in the past and present day African has been unsurpassed throughout history. During the foundation of America, Europeans tried to enslave other races including their own and Native Americans; however, they could not endure the brutality and pressures of slavery. It was due to the natural inner strength and aggression that existed in the African that enabled him to endure the brutal slave trade.

WILLINGNESS TO INFLICT CRUELTY

While Africans have a high aggression level, they have a very low will to inflict cruelty onto other races. For example, Caucasians in America formed hate organizations such as the KKK that persecuted and even mutilated and killed African Americans however, never in history has there ever been a black organization that terrorized and killed other races.

KNOWLEDGE OF RELIGION

"God gave us sex and we turn it into an ugly thing. God gave us religion and we turned it into an ugly thing. God gave us creation and we turn it into an ugly thing. We have turned against God and in turn God has turned against us!" (Minister Louis Farrakhan)

During slavery Africans were not allowed to worship or study religion. It was this act on behalf of the slave owner that has forever changed the lives of millions of African Americans.

Slavery contributed to the destruction of an entire people. Due to slavery Africans lost their identity and thus their religion. The quickest way to destroy a people is to destroy their religious belief. Let's face it; religion is the foundation of who we are. In most black families, the black man does not go to church. The male figure in all races is expected to lead. The black race is the only race of people where the woman is put in a position where she has to lead. She must raise the kids. She must teach the kids. She takes them to church. She is the leader.

Due to this lack of education of religion, black people don't understand the rules of God. They don't understand the inherent power that they can possess by performing this one act, creating a relationship with God. This is the reason that black men and women treat each other so badly. There is a tangible disconnect from God that has caused a distinct disconnect between the black man and black woman. They are subconsciously angry about their situation and they have nowhere else to focus it but on themselves.

KNOWLEDGE OF HISTORY

Not only do black people not understand their own history, they definitely don't understand the history of the world. Again this is largely due to slavery. From the moment the African was removed from Africa, there was no written record of history from the African perspective. For example, most African Americans cannot tell you what country their ancestors were from in Africa. The only history most African Americans know is the history they have been taught in European society. They do not understand the past so they can't plan for the future.

NATURAL PHYSICAL ABILITY

Africans and African descendents are by far the most physically dominant people in the history of the world. This is made obvious in the areas of sports entertainment such as running, boxing, football, baseball , singing etc… This theory is further proven by great entertainers such as Muhammad Ali, Mike Tyson, Michael Jordan, and Beyonce, etc…

RACIAL UNITY

For whatever reason, black people have not exhibited the ability to get along. As I stated earlier the continent of

Africa has been in turmoil for centuries. The African just like other races started out living in tribes just as have the European, the native American and other races. While tribes are a good sign of unity a people cannot become a dominant power with only tribal unity.

For Example, the Europeans lived for years in a tribal state. In other words for years they identified themselves as Anglos, Saxons, Vikings etc.. These were all tribes. Although very aggressive they could never become a world power until they formed nations such as England, France, etc.. The African however, although they live within boundaries that are identified as nations such as Nigeria, Ethiopia, Kenya, etc.. the majority of the people identify themselves by tribal origin. In other words, the inability to get along and the instability that exists in Africa was present long before the arrival of the Europeans. The American slave trade was made possible due to the very fact that African tribes sold other African war prisoners that had been captured to Europeans.

Despite the knowledge and physical domination Africans possess and despite the fact that they are from the wealthiest natural resource continent on the planet, they have not been able to come into power due to their inability to work together. In current times, Africans look at African Americans as inferior, stupid and lazy. African Americans typically look at Africans as snobbish and dishonest. This hatred exists amongst black people around the world including Kenyans, Hatians, and blacks from the Carribean. Unlike other races such as Italians, Jews and Hispanics, people of African descent tend to have a strong hatred for each other.

Black men whether justified or unjustified have lost the respect of the world but more importantly they have lost respect of themselves and also the respect of the black woman. Due to this lack of unity, every day in the life of an African and African American is typically full of anxiety.

BUSINESS SKILLS

Although African descendents have the ability to create money such as athletes and entertainment figures, they are unable to create wealth in the field of business as a whole. The comedian Chris Rock once said that there is not one black person in America that is wealthy. I thought he was wrong when he said it but it is true. Even the most successful African Americans such as Oprah Winfrey, Michael Jordan and Bill Cosby have not been able to achieve the level of business success like a Bill Gates, where their business success influences the world.

CHAPTER 13

THE EUROPEAN

KNOWLEDGE OF ENVIRONMENT

I don't think there is any doubt that the Europeans (hereafter referred to as Caucasians) have gone down in history as the greatest explorers in history. This characteristic was crucial in the rise of the Caucasian as the most dominant people in the history of the world. That is a characteristic that has stuck with them despite their departure from Europe. Even today I have noticed that Caucasians typically as a whole enjoy exploring diverse environments such as hiking, skiing deep sea diving more so than other races.

KNOWLEDGE OF SCIENCE

Caucasians possess a sort of curiosity that has never been seen before in history. They are always striving to understand the inherit laws of science that govern our Earth and our universe. They have created devices such as the automobiles, airplanes and modern medicine that make life easier for the world. But they also have used science to achieve power by creating powerful weapons of destruction that can kill millions in a matter of seconds.

Organization and Structure

Caucasians are typically very organized. They typically excel at setting up laws and systems of governments. They are known for writing long lasting great documents such as the Declaration of Independence and the Constitution. This skill is even expressed in Caucasian families. They are very big on structure of the family. They are constantly being taught structure from the role of the man in the household, how to manage money and how to plan for their future.

Aggression

Caucasians have throughout history shown aggression. The biggest example of this is the European's arrival in North America. The Europeans landed in North America and soon dominated the Native Americans by force.

Willingness to Inflict Cruelty

"Why have you killed people that didn't bother you? Why have you murdered people that opened their doors to you? Why have you murdered 100 million people for every thousand years of your existence on the planet? Therefore, you have killed more people than your own population. So if God were to take an eye for an eye and a tooth for a tooth and a life for a life... This is why doom is preached for the world of the white man! Because you have murdered all the

darker people of the Earth and you have earned your destruction!" Minister Louis Farrakhan.

These are pretty harsh words however; it is honestly how many races of the world view Caucasians due to their dominance and success and explains many nations view of America.

Caucasians have throughout history used violence to inflict their will on other races including their own in order to achieve domination. This has been expressed throughout history from the Romans during the Crusades, the British during the American Revolution; the Nazis during the holocaust; and even Americans during their initial arrival in the new world and the eventual destruction of the Native American and African American during the slave trade. Does this mean that white people are evil? No it doesn't. What is does mean is that they are willing to inflict violence when their security or financial domination is threatened.

This can be seen today in Iraq. Iraq a nation that never showed any aggression towards the United States was viciously attacked by the United States because the US felt as though one day they might become a threat.

Knowledge of Religion

Caucasians have a tremendous knowledge of religion. Although they might not display often times many of the principles of religion, they understand the importance of God in a races survival and domination. Religion is the foundation of which this nation was built. They even acknowledge God on their money. They have a tremendous understanding of the world and of the rules of God. For example, some of your most ruthless

Italian mafia gangsters pray and visit churches frequently. Although they understand what they are doing is wrong, they understand the rules of God and forgiveness. This supernatural characteristic strengthens them in life.

In addition they understand the power of religion in controlling a society. They are willing to rewrite history in order to maintain control of history. Let's look at a few examples.

Example Number 1: The Origin of the Cross

There once lived a great Roman ruler by the name of Constantine that decided that Christianity would be the official religion of Rome in 325 AD. Up until this point the symbol of Christianity was a fish. But Constantine is said to have had a vision that said the words "In hoc signo vinces" which translates from Latin to English as "With this sign we conquer." From that point forward, the Europeans used Christianity and the cross as a symbol to justifiably kill others and rule the world.

Example Number 2: Deleted Books of the Bible

Constantine also along with others at the council of Nicaea decided that they would delete books from the Bible. Did you know that there were additional books of the bible that were removed? Yes it's true! For example, there were additional books of the Bible that told the full story of the children of Adam and Eve. In other words, other books that tell the story of other children of Adam and Eve and how they were married. Romans were very against incest so they removed these books.

Example 3: The History of Easter

Constantine, although the emperor of Rome, was still a politician and upon him deciding Christianity to be the official religion of Rome wanted to please the bulk of the people. One of the largest religions in Rome at the time was Paganism. This was a Roman religion that worshipped the Sun. Every year the Pagans would worship Eastre, the Teutonic goddess of Spring and fertility. The Pagans would indulge in orgies and other sexual acts to reflect spring and fertility. A rabbit was used as the symbol because rabbits are very sexual animals and reproduce rapidly. This is why millions of Christians every year eat Easter eggs and buy Easter baskets. It had nothing to do with Jesus but everything to do with politics and tradition!

Example 3: The History of Christmas

Most historians will tell you that it is very unlikely that Jesus was born in December. The bible says that during the birth of Christ that the shepherds were abiding in the field tending flocks by night. In Palestine in December it is very cold. The sheep are typically in the barn due to the harsh winter. Again, here is another misconception due to the Pagonis tic society in order to get them to accept the Christian Religion.

Every year the sun worshippers saw the sun leaving them because the days were getting shorter and shorter. The sun wasn't actually moving of course the Earth was which is how we get different seasons and longer and shorter days. At any rate, when it got to the 21st day of December the sun appeared to stand still. It is the shortest day of the year and is called the Winter Solstice. Around this time (i.e. December 25th) the sun starts its journey back towards us and the Pagons called it the birth of the sun. While Christians are taught that this is the birth of Jesus the son of God it is actually a tradition of Pagan worshippers to reflect their worship of the solar sun.

The purpose of these examples was not to disregard Christianity or any other religion but rather to show that knowledge of religion means knowledge and control of the world and the Caucasian understands it and exploits it on a daily basis.

Knowledge of History

Not only do Caucasians have knowledge of their own culture's history. They study other society's history and culture. This is made apparent by the missionaries and explorers that travel the world not only to help other cultures but also to learn their way of life and their history.

Natural Physical Ability

This is an area where the Caucasian has a short coming as a whole. In other words, Caucasians are typically smaller framed people when compared to other races such as African and Hispanic. They have been known in history however to be very impressive athletes. For example the Olympic Games date back to Ancient Rome. As time progressed however, the Caucasian realized that true world domination would more likely be obtained through the other nine characteristics rather than through sports. Although the Caucasian still participates in sports heavily today, physical domination as a whole is not the focus of their community.

Racial unity

Caucasians have a tremendous ability to work together. They do tend to argue and fight amongst each other but they are still at the same time able to remain functional as whole. The self hatred and self destruction that exists among other races does not exist among the Caucasian.

Business skills

Caucasians are typically very good at making money. Not only are they able to use their strengths in science and mathematics for financial gain. They are able to use other races strengths to create financial gain. For example, an NFL owner will pay a black athlete millions per year for their physical ability so that they can make billions.

CHAPTER 14

THE HISPANIC

KNOWLEDGE OF ENVIRONMENT

Similar to the Africans, the Hispanic population has shown little interest in sailing or exploring new lands. What few people know however, is that much of the Hispanic environment was taken away from them. Did you know that what is currently Texas, Arizona and New Mexico was once the Mexican Territory. Mexicans are yet another race that has fallen at the hands of Europeans. It is kind of ironic that Hispanics in current day are no longer allowed to legally cross into what was once their homeland.

KNOWLEDGE OF SCIENCE

There is evidence that the Hispanic population had at one time a tremendous knowledge of science and astronomy. The Hispanics just like the Africans have displayed the ability to create great architectural structures such as pyramids on the South American continent. In addition the Mayans seemingly had a tremendous knowledge of astronomy and mathematics. When the Conquistadors (another European society) invaded their continent however, much of their scientific research was destroyed. In current times however, the Hispanic culture as a whole does not excel in the fields of science and mathematics.

Organization and Structure

Hispanics have also been unable to organize themselves in order to become a worldwide figure. Their governments are typically unstable and weak and their current structure has not proven capable to provide a comfortable lifestyle for their people. This is the main reason for the high rate of illegal immigration. It's not that they want to leave their homeland. The problem is that their homeland does not provide the structure and stability needed to survive comfortably.

Aggression

Hispanics have been gone down in history also as great warriors. Very similar to the Native Americans in North America once they were invaded by the Conquistadors, they lost much of their aggressive instinct.

Willingness to Inflict Cruelty

While Hispanics like other races were typically fierce warriors who fought great battles amongst each other. They never at any time have displayed the desire to inflict harm on nations abroad. In current society there have been incidents of aggression do to the tremendous increase in drug trafficking out of South America; however, they show little or no aggression towards any other races.

KNOWLEDGE OF RELIGION

The Conquistadors came through South America several hundred years ago and changed religion forever. Any written religion was destroyed. Due to this action the future of the Hispanic population has been forever changed. Again we find a people who have been separated from their natural religious beliefs and have thus had horrible effects.

KNOWLEDGE OF HISTORY

Hispanics typically do not have a good understanding of the history of the world. This is very much influenced to the fact that so much of their history has been destroyed by other cultures such as the Spanish.

NATURAL PHYSICAL ABILITY

Hispanics, very similar to Africans, tend to excel at entertainment such as boxing, singing, soccer etc.. In addition they tend to be incredibly honest hard working people that are willing to do labor intensive jobs that others are not willing to do.

RACIAL UNITY

Hispanics typically display a tremendous amount of cultural and racial unity.

Business skills

Hispanics tend to have a knack for business. Their only hold up is lack of opportunity. Even in the United States Hispanics have pooled their resources and have formed businesses, law firms and even banks.

CHAPTER 15

THE MIDDLE EASTERN

KNOWLEDGE OF ENVIRONMENT

The next race, who in my opinion is one of the most interesting people of the world, are the people of the Middle East. They are running neck and neck with the Caucasian in every way. They are typically very knowledgeable of their environment. They always have been! I recall as a child being captivated by old Sinbad movies and how exciting it was to see how these people who travelled to faraway lands to discover new things.

KNOWLEDGE OF SCIENCE

They have a tremendous knowledge of mathematics and science. They always have. The people of this area were among the first in the world to study the fields of mathematics, science and astrology. For hundreds of years their society dominated in this arena.

Organization and Structure

For many years the people of the Middle East dominated and had a very organized system of government. They were amongst the first society to form cities very similar to those found in New York. The amazing thing is that they were able to achieve this thousands of years ago. Although what we see today is the same instability that we see in the continent of Africa. How did this happen?

During the Crusades their society was destroyed by the Europeans. What we see today is the result of this defeat at the hands of Europeans. I still believe this is one of the major reasons people of this area have a lot of animosity for Europeans and especially the United States.

Aggression

Middle Easterners are typically very aggressive and they are afraid of nothing! They are even willing to give their life at a moment's notice for what they believe in. They were and are fierce warriors who typically don't fear anything other than God.

Willingness to inflict cruelty

What makes the United States as well as other powerful Nations of the world uncomfortable is the fact that out of all the races, Middle Easterners are one of the only races that is willing to inflict cruelty on other races to the extreme. They are typically indifferent who the casualties are in the time of war. Their only focus is winning. For example the September 11th bombing of the World Trade Center killed hundreds including women and children. The Middle Easterner is currently the only race willing to kill without discrimination and without remorse. This characteristic does make them strong however.

Knowledge of Religion

Despite the defeat at the hands of Europeans, they have preserved their religion and their customs. They have refused over the course of hundreds of years to assimilate. They are the only people in history that have been defeated at the hands of Europeans but have been able to preserve their way of life. They know who they are. They know God and have a tremendous respect for God. They know without a doubt the rules of their religion. They are very devoted to their religion and take it very seriously. The United States is currently in Iraq and Afghanistan trying to convert these people to our way of living and thinking. This is a very futile act on our behalf. These people would rather die than give up who they are!

Knowledge of History

Not only do the people of the Middle East understand their history, they understand the history of the world. In fact they are one of the only groups of people in world that can trace their lineage hundreds of years back.

Natural Physical Ability

The people of this area are typically not extremely physically impressive. They are typically smaller people whose strength typically comes through their ideas and thoughts not the physical.

Racial unity

Why they have fought amongst each other for thousands of years, they typically have a strong racial unity. This is displayed every day in Afghanistan. The United States has been trying to kill Osama Bin Laden for years. Our troops can never seem to capture him because of the racial unity in the area. The people of Afghanistan as well as the people of Pakistan will not give him up for any amount of money. This is a powerful characteristic that positions them for domination in the future.

Business skills

These people have a tremendous business mind. They too have been blessed with a continent rich with a natural resource that the world needs. That resource is of course oil. They expose this in the global market on a daily basis and in the process have made large amount s of money.

CHAPTER 16

JEWISH

KNOWLEDGE OF ENVIRONMENT

Jews were never known for being sailors however they have settled societies around the world. They can be found on each end of the world. For this reason, they have obtained a keen sense of their place in the world and in the universe.

KNOWLEDGE OF SCIENCE

Jews are a race that produced Albert Einstein, the inventor of the atom bomb! Shall we say more? Yes, Jews have a tremendous knowledge of mathematics and science!

ORGANIZATION AND STRUCTURE

Jews are typically very organized. They typically excel at setting up laws and systems of governments similar to Caucasians. They are also very big on structure of the family. Very similar to the Caucasians, Jews, are constantly teaching their children structure, how to manage money and how to function in the world.

AGGRESSION

Jews are typically not very aggressive unless they are forced to be. They have one of the strongest militaries in that area of the world.

WILLINGNESS TO INFLICT CRUELTY

Despite the atrocities that they have suffered from the Nazis and other races throughout the years, they have little desire to hurt other people. In fact they are known for their charity and acts of kindness around the world.

Due to their financial success however, they have been able to form an impressive military arsenal. When threatened however Jews are willing to defend themselves in a very aggressive manner.

KNOWLEDGE OF RELIGION

Jews are often called "God's chosen people" due to the stories of the Bible. Jews typically have a tremendous knowledge of religion. Not only do they have a knowledge of their own religion they are typically educated equally in the religion of others.

KNOWLEDGE OF HISTORY

Jews are typically very educated and have a tremendous knowledge of the world. In addition they are one of the few races that can trace their history for thousands of years. Jews can trace their history from Egypt where they were slaves through their long migration and eventual arrival in Israel.

Natural Physical Ability

Jews are typically not known for their physical characteristics. They are typically smaller in stature physically when compared to other races and show little interest in the areas of sports.

Racial Unity

Typically races that have been severely oppressed often have little racial unity due to the frustration they experience living in their environment. Despite the fact that Jews have in my opinion suffered more cruelty than any other race in history from slavery in Egypt to the Holocaust in Nazi Germany, they have a remarkable ability to get along. Many African Americans blame their current problems on slavery. This is true to a certain extent. But please remember, Jews were slaves in Egypt for over 400 hundred years. African Americans were slaves in America for only about 100 years.

What I think the Jews have shown is that no matter how much a race is oppressed and mistreated by others a race that is unified is unstoppable and can achieve anything.

Business Skills

Although the European might have conquered the world, the Jews run the world. They are the wealthiest race of people on the planet. They control the music industry, the movie industry television, the medical industry, etc.. Jews even own BET (Black Entertainment Television) and Essence magazine. The list goes on and on. Did you know that 25% percent of the doctors and lawyers in the United States are Jewish? Did you know that most of the professional sports owners in the United States are Jewish? Also most of the wealthy black people in the United States such as Oprah Winfrey, JZ, Bill Cosby and Michael Jordan have a Jew somewhere in their lives guiding their career.

Jews have always been good at making money. They are some of the most shroud business people ever. Many people don't realize that before the holocaust in Nazi Germany Jews were one of the most financially successful races of the world. It was largely due to this success throughout Europe that they became persecuted.

Despite their stressful past, Israel is one of the most modern countries of the world and have technology equivalent to that of the rest of the modern world.

Not only do they know how to make money they are extremely good at keeping it in the family and within their race. They work extremely well together as a race and are still considered as some of the most successful business people in the world. They own a tremendous portion of the wealth of the world.

Chapter 17

Asian

Knowledge of Environment

Asians were never great sailors either however their race has populated around the world. Due to this and their tremendous education they are very knowledgeable of their environment.

Knowledge of Science

Asians are typically very knowledgeable of math and science. They are running neck to neck with the rest of the world in advances in the field of math and science.

Organization and Structure

Asians are typically very organized. They are also good at setting up laws and systems of governments similar to Caucasians.

Aggression

Asians have throughout history been very aggressive. They have gone down in history as fierce warriors that are not afraid of anything.

Willingness to inflict cruelty

Asians are natural fighters and are willing to inflict cruelty or aggression on any race including their own that threaten them. This was made apparent during World War II when kamikaze pilots sacrificed their lives by flying airplanes into US ships.

Knowledge of religion

Asians are typically not as religious and spiritual as other races. While they do believe in God they are typically lead more by intellect than spirituality in decision making.

Knowledge of history

Asians are typically very big on history. They are very aware of their family's history and their culture's history.

Natural Physical Ability

Although they are typically small in stature, Asians have tremendous physical ability. They lead in several sports such as gymnastics, dancing and of course the martial arts.

Racial unity

Asians typically are typically able to work together very well. They do not however, have the cohesiveness of races such as Jews.

BUSINESS SKILLS

Asians are very good at business. This is their primary focus in life, making money. There are numerous examples of this such as the tremendous amount of merchandise that is exported from Asia to the rest of the world and also the numerous small businesses Asians have throughout the world.

CHAPTER 18

THE NATIVE AMERICAN

KNOWLEDGE OF ENVIRONMENT

Chris rock said "I have seen a polar bear ride a unicycle but I have never seen eight Indians in the same room!"

Most people never do see eight Native Americans in one room because they have been isolated by America on reservations. The story of Native Americans is one of the most tragic stories in the history of America. Native Americans had a tremendous respect for their environment. Before the arrival of Europeans they lived very much in harmony with nature. Despite their respect for their environment they have never had the desire to migrate outside their environment.

KNOWLEDGE OF SCIENCE

Native Americans have never been known to pursue the sciences. There focus has always been that of a more spiritual nature with the belief that the Earth would always take care of their needs.

Organization and Structure

Upon the arrival of the Europeans, Native American structure was destroyed. Despite their simple way of life, pre European arrival Native Americans actually had communities set up. Due to the vicious acts by Europeans such as violent attacks and slavery on Native Americans there structure was destroyed! Unfortunately, they have through the years never been able to recover. Today they live on reservations where their society has been stripped of everything and they are plagued with personal issues such as depression and alcoholism.

Aggression

The Native American was once one of the greatest natural warriors in the history of the world. However, since their conquer at the hands of Europeans, Native Americans have shown little to no aggression towards their oppressors or any other race.

Willingness to Inflict Cruelty

The Native Americans have shown little desire to inflict harm on any races throughout the years.

Knowledge of Religion

Native Americans were stripped of their religion similar to African Americans. This is yet another factor that has weekend their society.

Knowledge of history

While Native Americans typically have a tremendous knowledge of their own history but have little interest in other societies.

Natural Physical Ability

Native Americans are typically impressive in stature.

Racial unity

Native Americans are typically unified however they don't translate this unification into progression in the outside world. The Native American very similar to Africans have always organized themselves in tribes. Even today, most Native Americans identify themselves as members of a tribe. As I stated earlier domination in the world can not be obtained while living in a tribal state. True domination can only be formed by forming nations.

Business skills

Native Americans have through the years have not excelled in the field of business outside the reservations. They have over the past years tried to form small businesses and casinos around the country. It has not yet been proven if this attempt will be successful.

CHAPTER 19

EUROPEAN ROAD TO DOMINATION

As I stated earlier, the European culture has indeed dominated the world. From the Romans to the British Empire and even now the United States, the Caucasian race has managed to stay ahead of other races in society. As the domination chart reflects, they score a whopping 94 out of a possible 100. The only two areas of weakness are physical attributes and the willingness to inflict cruelty. While physical ability in current times has very little effect on a races success the willingness to inflict cruelty does. Caucasians scored a score of 9 in this category however the Middle Eastern races scored a 10. Why the difference in score?

For example, terrorists bombed the world trade center in 2001 without hesitation killing hundreds of innocent people including children. Caucasians whether in the US, England or France would never do such an act! If you look at the Middle Eastern races they scored a 10. There total score was 92 only a few points lower than the Caucasian.

In order for the Caucasian to remain in power he must keep this characteristic on an as needed basis. In other words, he must never mistreat people who are not a threat but be willing to be unusually cruel to those who are. For example in the Afghanistan and Iranian war US soldiers are constantly complaining that they cannot effectively fight the war due to the United States policy on how to treat the enemy. America has lost this killer instinct that is needed at times. If Europeans do not recapture this characteristic their global power will be in jeopardy.

CHAPTER 20

AFRICAN ROAD TO DOMINATION

The biggest problem in the African community worldwide is lack of organization, lack of unity, lack of religion and lack of business skills. The Jews have shown that slavery or even an incident such as the holocaust cannot keep a united and organized race oppressed.

The first area needed for domination is religion. Black people need to become educated on the rules of life and they need to be taught the rules of God! They have become so caught up in the pain and misery of the natural they can't see the power of the supernatural!

Again, black people don't understand the inherent supernatural power that they already possess by having a relationship with God. The religious foundation amongst African and African Americans must be rebuilt. They need to understand that by doing so they can accomplish great things such as other races. By emphasizing religion, organization and unity will automatically fall into place.

In the area of business, Africans in particular African Americans have made tremendous strides. A race of people who only a few hundred years ago were slaves now has several businesses, professional athletes and even a black president of the United States. Despite the fact that the African American race has several success stories, the fact remains that most Africans and African Americans around the world live at or below the poverty level. Why is this?

As I stated earlier, African American Americans such as Michael Jordan, Bill Cosby and Oprah Winfrey have reached multimillionaire status; the fact remains African Americans as a whole have no financial wealth. How is this possible?

The problem is they don't have a product that the world needs! For example Michael Jordan is worth approximately 500 million dollars but his wealth was achieved because of his ability as a professional athlete. Bill Cosby a tremendous comedian and actor has made millions due to his entertainment ability. Oprah Winfrey has made hundreds of millions as a talk show host and actress. Despite the fact they also became excellent business people later; their opportunities were created because of entertainment. In addition, despite their success they don't have nearly enough wealth to change the overall status of their race.

In my opinion it would be in the best interest of the African race over the next 100 years to become producers. Not only producers of records, sport events, videos and movies. The real money is in producing a product that the world needs! For example, despite the fact that I am a huge Michael Jordan fan, let's face it the world can do without basketball! And as much as I love Oprah and Bill Cosby, the world can do without entertainment and talk shows. As I stated earlier, the Caucasian realized thousands of years ago that world domination could not be based off of entertainment. In addition, just as the Romans eventually lost interest in entertainment, it is very likely the technology based world we live in today will soon not place the emphasis on sports and entertainment like we do today. Do you remember only 20 years ago sit comes such as The Cosby Show, Different Strokes and the Jeffersons where top rated shows? This trend has changed. There are very few sitcoms now. Reality shows are the focus now! Our society is changing from an entertainment society to a reality and technology based society. What would happen if the world decided not to pay entertainers millions? While other races would maintain their power it would deeply affect the hopes and dreams on so many African American children that idealize entertainers.

While the world can do without entertainment, the world cannot however live without oil, other forms of energy, computers, communication, electricity, medicine, etc.. What Africans and African Americans need is a product! More specific, they need a product that the world is dependent on in order to achieve wealth. This would give them financial power, also respect and dignity in the world and thus change the life of the race as a whole.

For example Bill Gates is worth approximately 50 billion dollars. That's 100 times the wealth of Michael Jordan, Oprah or Bill Cosby. The reason he was able to obtain this wealth is the fact that he has a product that the world needs! His computer system runs the world! Not only has he changed his life he has made several millionaires that work for him. In addition he has hundreds of thousands that work for him directly or indirectly to sell his product. The Middle Easterner has a product (i.e. oil) that is needed by the world. They are then able to help each other because they as a race are a producer. This is the definition of true wealth!

While I applaud Oprah, Michael Jordan and Bill Cosby because of their achievements, I think it would be wise to use the money obtained through entertainment in order to achieve true wealth. Wouldn't it be great if the wealthiest Africans and African Americans in world united, pooled their resources and invested in Africa the wealthiest continent in the world! Wouldn't it be great if this wealth could be used to organize Africa and enable it to live up to its full potential? Africa is full of diamonds, gold, oil and other valuable natural resources.

Even if the investment is not done in Africa, African Americans need to try to become a producer of something the world needs. This could be anything from an alternative energy source to a medicine that cures AIDS.

If people of African descent around the world could somehow unite they would without a doubt become the most dominant race in the history of mankind!

CHAPTER 21

JEWISH ROAD TO DOMINATION

The Jewish race is the only race that is content with their place in the world. Jews are a people who know who they are and have defined what their goals are in life. They have learned how to achieve wealth and also spiritual peace.

Chapter 22

Hispanic road to domination

The Hispanic race is a race of beautiful spirited people and inherently hard workers. The media exploits the behavior of Hispanics that have come to America illegally and also the drug cartel in Mexico. What the world must understand is that all of these acts have been done in order to survive. The life of the average South American is well below poverty level. I myself cannot say that I would not do the same if I felt that there was no hope.

What it would take in order to change the lifestyle of Hispanic nations is a global effort on behalf of many nations to better the lifestyle of Hispanics. Very similar to the relief effort in Haiti after the great earth quake, South America needs the help of the nations of the rest of the world to achieve their potential. This would prevent the immigration problem that has been so widely publicized. If the people had something to stay for they wouldn't flee their homeland.

They also need to be educated in the fields of mathematics and science so that they may become producers like other nations of the world.

CHAPTER 23

ASIAN ROAD TO DOMINATION

The Asian population such as China are often called sleeping giants. They are called this because the world knows they have tremendous potential to become a super power due to their knowledge of science their organizational skills and the fact they are producers to the world. This is race is destined for a role as a true super power.

CHAPTER 24

MIDDLE EASTERN ROAD TO DOMINATION

The Middle Eastern race is the biggest threat to the long lasting reign of the Caucasian. Middle Eastern races rank just as high or higher as all other races on the domination chart in almost every category. The only thing they lack is organization. This area is also known for unstable governments and war. If they ever become organized they would actually score as high as the Caucasian overall! The Caucasian understands this which is why they constantly monitor their activities. Recently, the United States has placed a noticeable emphasis on intelligence and electronic commerce. This is due to the fact that Middle Easterners are trying to become organized and thereafter would become a superpower. For example, the CIA has learned that it takes an incredible amount of money to create a nuclear weapon, so they constantly monitor the transfer of money around the world. The Middle Easterner has the knowledge of how to create such a weapon however due to the electronic intelligence of the Caucasion he can not move the money to build it. The Middle Easterner must be careful however not to become too aggressive however, or the world as a whole will feel threatened and then will unite and ultimately destroy their civilization very similar to the Japanese during World War II.

CHAPTER 25

NATIVE AMERICAN ROAD TO DOMINATION

In order for the Native American to prosper their entire society must undergo a total rebuilding process. The United States owes it to this race to help them to rebuild. They need education in the areas of science. They need organizational structure. They need money so they can improve their life style. A once brilliant and beautiful people have now been reduced to a race of high rates of alcoholism and depression. They understand very well that they have limited opportunities and possibilities. America will never live up to her full potential until this gross misdeed has been undone.

Chapter 26

Road to Domination Conclusion

I know there will be detractors of this book who will call it racist and stereotypical. Please be reminded that this book was not meant to insult or demean any race. I know it is full of generalizations and I know that an entire race can not be stereotyped. What I was attempting to do with this book it point out overwhelming characteristics of each race that explain their current situation in the world. I also wanted to point out that since the beginning of time races have risen and lost their power in this world due to these characteristics discussed in this book. Usually a society has global domination for only about 500 years and then another race dominates.

It just points out what many people already know is true but the world doesn't know how to say it. What I hope this book does show is the huge possibilities of man as a whole. That by focusing on each of the principles stated that any people regardless of race are capable of dominating their fate as well as dominating the world.